Felicia C. Lucas

THE BOUNCE BACK

Triumphant Stories of Resiliency and Perseverance

FOREWORD BY:
Sharlrita Deloatch

Pearly Gates Publishing, LLC, Houston, Texas

The Bounce Back

The Bounce Back:
Triumphant Stories of
Resiliency and Perseverance

Copyright © 2017
Felicia C. Lucas

All Rights Reserved.
No portion of this publication may be reproduced, stored in any electronic system, or transmitted in any form or by any means (electronic, mechanical, photocopy, recording, or otherwise) without written permission from the author or publisher. Brief quotations may be used in literary reviews.

Some names and identifying details have been changed to protect the privacy of individuals.

ISBN 13: 978-1-945117-92-3
ISBN 10: 1-945117-92-3
Library of Congress Control Number: 2017956450

Scripture references are used with permission from Zondervan via Biblegateway.com.

For information and bulk ordering, contact:
Pearly Gates Publishing, LLC
Angela R. Edwards
P.O. Box 62287
Houston, TX 77205
BestSeller@PearlyGatesPublishing.com

Felicia C. Lucas

Dedication

This book is dedicated to individuals who are facing the biggest storms of their lives and are seeking some inspiration in order to make it through.

The Bounce Back

Bounce Back Authors' Acknowledgements

Minister Felicia Lucas:

To my Lord and Savior Jesus Christ: Thank You so much for blessing me with the desire to share my life story with the world. To Kelvin, the best husband a woman can have: I love you so much. You always keep pushing me towards my best possible. To my children (Isaiah, Kelsey, and Silas), family, and friends: Thanks for your unending support. To my Spiritual Daughter: You are a phenomenal poet. Keep allowing God to speak to you through poetry. To Pearly Gates Publishing and Angela Edwards: I am eternally grateful for this opportunity to be a part of your family. Thank you, Stevii Aisha Mills and Dr. Marilyn E. Porter, for making this connection possible. To my Co-Authors and Foreword Writer: Thank you so much for saying "YES!" to this project. I am so proud of each of you!

****

Pastor Shamielle Alston:

To God: Thank You for loving me enough to allow me to travel life's journey! To Felicia Lucas: Thank you for allowing me to be a part of this phenomenal project. I am immensely grateful! To those who have/are struggling with faith: God sees you, He cares, and yes, He has a plan. Trust Him and walk into your greatness!

****

Felicia C. Lucas

Melissa Bridgers-Allen:

I would like to thank God for believing in me when I didn't have faith in myself. To Pastor Jonah Walston, Jr. and my son, Jay who never complained and to every individual and family member who played a part in my life to help Melissa find herself. Last, but not least, to my husband and soulmate, Montie, for being that man who understood me from the club to the church house.

> *"Such things were written in the Scriptures long ago to teach us. The Scriptures give us hope and encouragement as we wait patiently for God's promises to be fulfilled"*
> (Romans 15:4, NLT).

****

Louvanta White:

I would like to take this moment to show my love and gratitude to those who have been on this journey with me. First and foremost, I want to give all honor and praises unto God. If it wasn't for Him instilling the gifts in me, this wouldn't be possible. I want to thank my wonderful family, my SESI family, my UPS family, my Friends, and I can't forget our visionary behind this whole project. Thank you all so much. God bless you all!

****

The Bounce Back

Elder Lorrie Crawley:

This chapter is a result of two journeys of faith, trust, and healing. Like so many other things in my life, this accomplishment would not have been possible if it weren't for key people in my life. I am appreciative of my husband, Robert Crawley, Sr., who gave his quiet strength, support, and love. I heard you loud and clear. To my children: Kitara (who has completed her journey), Robert Jr., and Kaylom. To my siblings who were strength in my journey. To my mother, Virginia Hawkins; a true example of strength under pressure. To my Daddy God who carried me every step of my journey.

****

Rayshoun Chambers:

At a time when so much joy was on the verge of being overshadowed by the spirit of doubt, my beliefs stood firm. Glory to God for being my Ever-After, my Protector, and Provider. I want to thank all of my friends, family, and hilarious coworkers who were there during my pregnancy for all of your support, pulling together, working hard to ensure the smile I had was the smile I kept. To my mother, Joanne Smaw-Asomugha, my father, Phil Chambers, and siblings, Lord Michael Chambers, John Gaines, and Corey Chambers: I love you. To my son, Cameron Lewis Chambers: God has already gifted you with so much. I love you always.

****

Felicia C. Lucas

Malissa Stringer:

I am grateful for the love and continual support of my personal mentor, Sheila Greene, who has been a mother, sister, friend, and confidant all wrapped up in one. Thank you for never missing an important date. Last, but certainly not least, my children, Kris and Alex, for always pushing me during the tough times. I love you guys! This one is for you! Words could never express what you mean to me.

****

Nena B. Abdul-Wakeel:

Thank you, Lord, for being the Strong Tower and Comforter in my life, particularly through my grief journey. I particularly want to thank four special angels in my life who supported me in this "new thing" called 'writing': My mother, Zaimah A, who unconditionally loves and supports me; Edna O. and DeAndrea D. for holding me up and pushing me forward when I doubted; and Christine W. who set an example and showed me that I could share my story in words. Lastly, to my sons Khalil and Malek, for always being in my corner.

****

~ x ~

The Bounce Back

DuWanda S. Epps:

I must give thanks to Christ my Savior because all things are possible through Christ who is my Strength and Redeemer. I am thankful for all the people I have unknowingly inspired throughout the years and even today. To my loved-ones, few close friends, and my supporters: Thank you for believing in me. I will be forever thankful.

****

Sharlrita Deloatch:

I want to thank God for allowing me to go through all that I've been through to help someone else and allow me to still be alive in the process to tell the story. Thank you to my wonderful husband, Anthony, and my beautiful children for always supporting me. I am grateful for all of my family and the many lives that will be changed by this book. A special 'Thank You' to my sister in business and life, Felicia Lucas, for thinking of me to be a part of her #1 Best-Selling book project.

> *"Shout with the voice of a trumpet blast. Shout aloud! Don't be timid. Tell my people Israel of their sins!"*
> (Isaiah 58:1, NLT)

Felicia C. Lucas

The Bounce Back

FOREWORD

By: Sharlrita Deloatch

We often hear the quote, "*What doesn't kill you makes you stronger*". I say it **has** to make you stronger if God allows you to still be here while going through "it". Whatever your "it" is, it's only there to make you stronger.

For many years, I tried to run away from telling my story. I didn't want everyone to read or hear about that 'bad thing' Sharlrita did. I felt ashamed and embarrassed. Some of my family are used to the jail, probation, and being in and out of court; but when it happened to me, I thought I was just carrying on the family tradition — until I had my "coming to Jesus" moment while sitting in a holding cell awaiting my mom and stepdad to come bail me out. I made a decision to not allow "this" to stop or hinder me. I made a decision to not come back to this place again.

Fast-forward to 2014. I decided to tell and write my story — just like these ladies here. However, I told the **wimpy** story. I told the same story like every other woman who ever dealt with self-esteem issues. God said, **"No: Tell the truth... the WHOLE truth!"** From 2014 until today, I boldly tell my story of

Felicia C. Lucas

being a convicted felon in the state of North Carolina to being a thriving Woman Entrepreneur, helping women like me and those who desire to use their purpose to turn it into a business with a solid foundation. That's what you call a **"Bounce Back"**!

Just like these women in this book, you will read how they took their pain and *'Bounced Back'*. You will read stories of bouncing back from sickness, brokenness, and all of the pitfalls that we find in life.

Read and congratulate these women for taking the bold step to write their stories so that others can be healed.

The Bounce Back

INTRODUCTION

Over the course of my life, I have often thought about the story of Job in the Bible. Job was an upright man who experienced extreme levels of adversity in his life, to include losing everything he was closely-connected to. Even as he was going through his experiences, he had a tremendous level of faith and even expressed it to God by saying in Job 13:15 (KJV), "*Though he slay me, yet will I trust in him.*" Now, that is a powerful statement! At the end of the story, Job was able to **'Bounce Back'** — and gained more than he had lost!

Have you ever gone through something in life that shook the very core of your existence? Have you ever lost something or someone who was very close to you? Have you experienced such a treacherous situation and had no clue if and when you would make it through? Have you ever given a lot in a relationship or to a company and were abruptly let go?

My vision for this book was to share triumphant stories of individuals from all over who had different stories but were able to survive and wanted to share how they **'Bounced Back and Persevered'**. I wanted women who had experienced molestation, incest, rape, death, poverty, divorce, betrayal,

Felicia C. Lucas

fired, repossession, miscarriage, abortion, bankruptcy, suicidal attempts, abuse, church hurt, cancer, or domestic violence to come together and share how they were able to make it through!

I was blessed to connect with a group of phenomenal women who have experienced different stories but had one thing in common: God brought them through some very dark places in life and they were able to overcome—just as I did! My desire is this: As you read each of our stories, you are inspired and encouraged to hang on and know that out there in this world, there is someone who has a similar experience and ultimately **'Bounced Back'**!

One of my Spiritual Daughters captures the essence of resiliency and expresses her personal 'Bounce Back' story through the following literary interpretation.

I introduce to some and present to others:
'The Sway Poet'

The Bounce Back

"A Heart of a Rose"

I guess you can compare my life right now
to a rose blooming in the Spring.
I see new sights, new beginnings, and I'm reaching new levels;
But just a few months ago, where my very heart laid,
was getting stepped on.
Trampled by people who I thought loved to see me bloom.
They would stare in amazement
and point out all the beauty they saw;
But the moment I began to wither and die,
they no longer saw my importance.
So, I disappeared. I faded into the dirt.
I blend well with it because I begin to
turn brown from the inside out.
My heart rots from the sheer disappointment
their eyes speak at the sight of me.
It turns out I'm not as pretty as they thought.
It turns out I'm not as strong as my story shows me to be.
It turns out I get weak, too.
So, they forget me until they begin to see the sun again.
They look for me when my stem has strengthened
And the smell of me brings bees and honey.
They see me when the sunlight shines
on the petals of my skin.
Oh, now you see me!
Well, these last few months I've refused
to focus on how you see me.
My priorities shifted while I was enduring
this extremely cold Winter.
I tried everything to feel some kind of warmth.
The only place I could feel it was when I looked
beyond the sun to the heavens.
So, now I'm blooming. I'm strengthening and
stretching to reach You, God.
I plan to grow as far as You allow.
And when my Winter comes again,
I will still embrace the warmth you bring.

The Bounce Back

TABLE OF CONTENTS

DEDICATION	VI
BOUNCE BACK AUTHORS' ACKNOWLEDGEMENTS	VII
FOREWORD	XIII
INTRODUCTION	XV
I DIDN'T KNOW MY OWN STRENGTH	1
MY TUNNEL OF GRIEF	11
THE TWO JOURNEYS	19
BOUNCING BACK AFTER A PERSONAL LOSS (RESOURCE CHAPTER)	27
AGAINST ALL ODDS	45
FORGIVENESS LED ME TO LOVE	53
I AM A STRIVER, BELIEVER, AND CONQUEROR!	59
THE GIRL WHO MATURED TOO FAST	67
AWAKENED	75
STILL YES!	83
THE BOUNCE BACK AUTHORS' BIOS	91
REFLECTIONS (JOURNALING SECTION)	102

Felicia C. Lucas

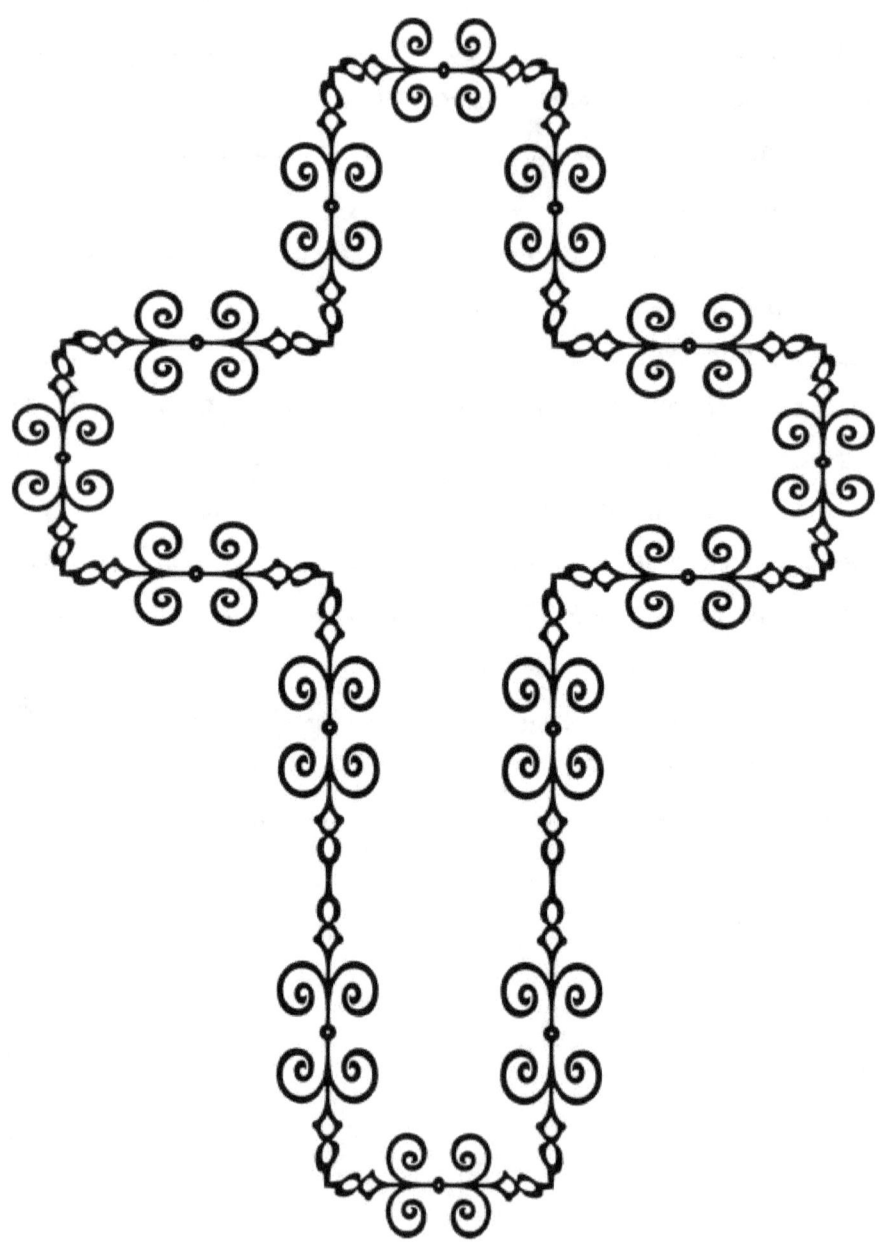

I Didn't Know My Own Strength
By: Minister Felicia Lucas

As I look back over my life, there are several situations that I have experienced in which I didn't know how strong I actually was. There have been many times (as I was going through) I knew it was God who carried me. I am sharing two specific times in my life when He gave me the strength to persevere. I pray these experiences encourage your faith in Him.

A Letter to My Unborn Seed:

I carry a tiny 3x2 card in my wallet which reads: *"In loving memory of Baby Lucas. 6-2-2000. We celebrate your short life. As we grieve over your loss, we know that your spirit is with God and one day we will meet. Even though we only knew of you for a short time, you will always remain in our hearts. Love, your parents!"*

It was very difficult to share with your siblings about your existence. In their young minds and fragile hearts, they found it hard to comprehend the thought of losing a sibling they never met. At Christmas, we hang a stocking for you to remind us of what had occurred. I sometimes wonder how I was able to bounce back after experiencing a miscarriage, but with God's help and the love and support of your father, I was able to do so.

I remember sitting on the edge of my bed waiting to see the results of my pregnancy test. I had started feeling nauseous and my upper chest area was quite sore. I recognized my monthly cycle was late and I was most likely pregnant. Your older brother was six months old at the time. I anxiously went to the restroom and looked at the results. It read that I was **POSITIVELY PREGNANT**. I was so *excited*! I waited until your father came home from work to share the news with him. We were going to be parents again! I was *ecstatic*! I remember telling him the news — and he was happy, too! I immediately contacted my OB/GYN to set up my prenatal appointment.

The day of the appointment finally came. They took bloodwork and a urine sample. My doctor confirmed the pregnancy test. We left the doctor's office so excited about the next leg of our parental journey. I immediately called a close friend to share the news with her. She was happy for me as well. All of that week, I was getting used to the fact that we were expecting. On that Friday, I started to spot, so I called my doctor. I had to go to the office for another appointment. His office then informed me that I had a 'Spontaneous Abortion'. I remember saying to the nurse, **"No. I didn't have an abortion!"**

I Didn't Know My Own Strength

She explained to me that I was experiencing a miscarriage. I can't even begin to put into words the thoughts I was having.

Did I do something to cause this?

Was God punishing me for something?

Am I a bad mother?

Why, God? Why?

The initial shock of the experience gradually faded. I then became sad. Sad to never have met you. Sad to see the look on my husband's face. Sad that your brother would not have you in his life.

The "Serenity Prayer" — *'God, grant me the serenity to accept the things that I cannot change, the courage to change the things I can, and the wisdom to know the difference'* — was very real for me during this time in my life. Slowly…ever so slowly…I began to bounce out of the sadness.

One day, my husband said to me, "*We still have our oldest child*". He was so right! Yes, we experienced a loss but we still had a perfectly healthy six-month-old son who still needed his parents. In that moment, things changed and I began to focus on who was here. It was okay to be sad but it was vital that I shifted mentally so I could be there for my son. We were thankful for this opportunity to be chosen as parents. If God allowed us to conceive again, that would be wonderful!

Fourteen months following the miscarriage, we conceived again. We were so happy! We did not tell anyone of the pregnancy until we were almost three months. I was so afraid of miscarrying again, so I was cautious about everything during the pregnancy. At the time, I did not have any pregnancy health insurance—which meant I had to self-pay at my doctor's office. They set me up on a sliding scale for the physician's bill. We were able to pay the required amount prior to the delivery. I went into labor and delivery with the anxiety of knowing this huge hospital medical bill will be ours to pay after the birth.

God blessed us with a healthy baby girl and we were ecstatic! The hospital bill ended up being **over $20,000**. We did not have that kind of money. I just knew the payment arrangements that the hospital would propose to be paid monthly would be expensive. I reluctantly called the hospital to speak with the representative in accounts. They pulled up my account and told me I did not have a balance. I asked, "*Are you sure?*" They stated my account had been cleared! No balance due! Praise God! He made a way!

I Didn't Know My Own Strength

To my unborn seed: I often wonder what you would have been when you grew up, what your favorite food would be, and if you would have liked sports as much as your siblings. I know our family dynamics would be quite different as a family of six rather than five. The reality of not knowing you has gotten better over time. You see: God helped us 'Bounce Back'! Because of my faith in Him, I know I will meet you one day. Until then, I love you forever! Mom.

****

I Didn't See This One Coming:

I remember the last time I saw you. It was at a family gathering. If I had known it was my final time, I would have hugged you much longer.

Fast-forward two months later. I remember you and I on a phone call that Sunday afternoon. You told me you weren't feeling well. Two days later, I was informed you had to be airlifted to a hospital in a nearby city because you were very sick. I had no idea you wouldn't pull through. In my mind, I had told myself that one day, you and I would reminisce about your hospital stay and I would say to you, "*Yes, you were real sick but look how God healed you!*" In actuality, God **did** heal you — but it was not the healing I **wanted**.

Felicia C. Lucas

I was asked to sing at your funeral. Boy, was I nervous, sad, and honored—all rolled up into one! I had rehearsed my piece acapella and was prepared to sing it that way but the church had an organist who immediately found my key and accompanied me musically. I selected a most appropriate song for the occasion, which is sung by Beverly Bam Crawford: *My Help*. I belted the words of the song from deep within my belly as God gave me the overwhelming strength to sing:

> *"I will lift up mine eyes to the hills*
> *From whence cometh my help;*
> *My help cometh from the Lord.*
> *The Lord which made Heaven and Earth.*
> *He said He will not suffer thy foot,*
> *Thy foot to be moved,*
> *The Lord that keepeth thee.*
> *He will not slumber nor sleep,*
> *For the Lord is thy keeper;*
> *The Lord is thy shade.*
> *Upon thy right hand, Upon thy right hand;*
> *No, the sun shall not smite thee by day,*
> *Not the moon by night.*
> *He shall preserve thy soul,*
> *Even forevermore.*
> *My help, my help, my help;*
> *All of my help cometh from the Lord."*

Even after the funeral, the words of that song brought me tremendous comfort. I would ride in my car with the CD on

I Didn't Know My Own Strength

'repeat' as the words would resonate within my heart. There were days I was sad…and there were days I was mad. Mad I couldn't just pick up the phone and talk to you about something I was experiencing. I was sad you were only 44 years old when you transitioned. I wanted you to be around to see my children grow up. I wanted to continue our many conversations on how to be a better parent which, by the way, you were great at. There were days I would call your phone just to hear your voice on the answering machine. I wanted to share with you my life's successes and the things I was going through.

I was left with a huge void in my life and for a couple of years following your death, I struggled tremendously. I didn't want to do anything, especially those things related to ministry. I went to the doctor and they could not find anything medically wrong with me. I took many tests and saw several specialists. Each would refer me to someone else. In the end, it was determined I was suffering from mild depression. With my doctor's help, the support of my husband, and the help of God, I overcame it.

Even as I am writing this chapter on July 16, 2017, I just received notice that your mother has just transitioned. This news opens up those hurts and pains I faced when you passed away. Your mother truly loved you and was very proud of all of the things you had accomplished in your life. The giving and serving side of you were qualities you got from her. After your death, she and I would talk on the phone. Talking to her kept my memories of you very close.

One thing about when a person 'Bounces Back' in a situation: It can be easy to go back to that previous state. As Gospel Artist, Pastor Marvin Sapp, sings about God in his song, *Never Would Have Made It*:

> "*Never would have made it;*
> *Never could have made it without You.*
> *I would have lost it all,*
> *But now I see how You were there for me and I can say:*
> *I'm stronger. I'm wiser.*
> *I'm better; much better.*
> *When I look back over all you brought me through,*
> *I can see that You were the One I held on to!*"

The same God who helped me back then will be the same God who will help me right now. This time, I am even stronger and I am in a better place in life! This, too, will be a testimony of **RESILIENCY** and **PERSEVERANCE**!

"Hear my cry, O God;
Attend unto my prayer.
From the end of the earth will
I cry unto Thee,
when my heart is overwhelmed:
lead me to the rock
that is higher than I."

Psalm 61-1-2

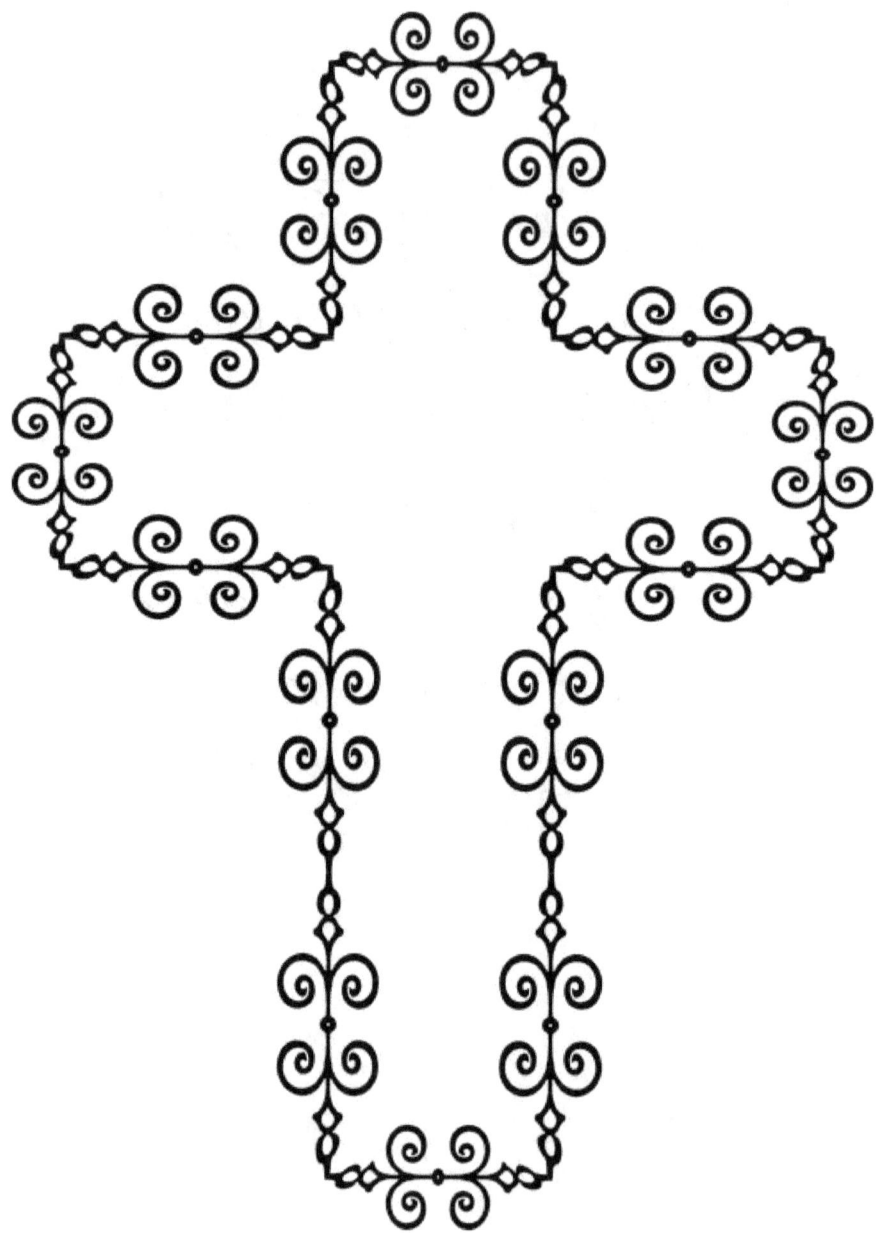

My Tunnel of Grief
By: Nena B. Abdul-Wakeel

On Wednesday, February 16, 2016, I received a call at about 9:00 p.m. The voice said, *"Nena, he's gone."* *"Who's gone?" "Eric's gone." "What happened?" "He died from a broken heart."*

At that moment, my heart **broke**. Eric, my ex-husband, the father of my children, and the love of my life was gone.

I have two sons, Khalil and Malek (then ages 14 and 8). Wednesday is children's and youth choir rehearsal night. It was late and my two sons and I were part of the last groups to leave after rehearsal was over. As the boys were getting into the car, I received the call. I remember slumping to the ground in shock. I could hear someone talking about the police investigator and saying something about me being the next of kin. This was not a dream…

Although his death was unexpected, I would be lying if I said I was surprised. Why? I knew he was sick from the last time I saw him which was about a week before. The Sunday before his death, I got a call that he was refusing to go to the doctor's office (he never liked doctors or needles). I called and talked to him. I got the typical response that I was nagging him and that nothing was wrong; however, I sensed in my spirit that something was very wrong. I prayed and asked God for help.

Who could I call? Who could influence him to go to the hospital?

I never reached anyone. I prayed. I cried. I was scared. I didn't know what to do. I prayed and the Spirit told me to "**JUST STOP!** *There is nothing you can do. Just prepare yourself to deal with what will come for you and the boys.*" I could only cry more.

After years of having a close relationship with God and hearing His voice, I knew I was clearly getting the message. Something bad was going to happen…and it did.

Three days later, Eric died from Diabetic Ketoacidosis.

Like anyone suddenly hit with grief, I was numb. For weeks, I was numb. I was responsible for handling all of the arrangements. He was an only child and his mother had passed away several years before. I guess the good and bad thing was I didn't have to coordinate the arrangements with anyone. His family from North Carolina was supportive but the decisions fell on me. Looking back, I don't know how I organized the funeral and got him buried in another state without breaking

My Tunnel of Grief

down. I guess that shows just how numb I was. **BUT** when the dam burst, I was a *MESS*!

When the emotions hit, it felt like someone physically reaching into my chest and **RIPPED** my heart out. I felt physical pain. It was so bad, all I could say was "*OH, GOD!*" — over and over and over again. For days, I wanted to just stay in bed under the covers in the dark. The only reason I couldn't was because of my children. I had to help them. They had just lost their father. How do you raise two Black boys without their father? All I could do was pray: "*God, help me.*"

During the day, I pulled myself together enough to take care of the boys and go to work. I did a lot of telework days because I couldn't face people. Talking about it and hearing condolences seemed to make the wound hurt more. I started trying to make myself feel better with wine. Every night for weeks, wine was my nighttime companion. I was never much of a drinker; just socially. But this? It wasn't social. For me, it was survival. Wine and food were my comforters. I gained about 15 pounds as I tried to fill the hole in my chest. It really didn't help. The weight gain made me more depressed.

Yes, I acknowledge I was depressed. I felt like the light in my spirit was turned all the way down. I knew I should still be praying—and I did…sometimes. Deep in my spirit, I knew that only God could help me get out of the pain and grief tunnel. Through it all, I felt God's hand of provision and comfort. I was getting help from people whom I never expected and in ways that **ONLY GOD** could organize. It helped to know that God was there and I believed He had plans for us.

Still… I was depressed. I realized I had to stop fighting the pain in order to be healed. I knew I needed to talk it out. I talked to a wonderful Spiritual Healer and Coach who was also a close friend. I told her I felt like I was in a tunnel. I was deep in the tunnel but could see a light. I felt like I was slowly crawling towards the light. I knew I had to deal with all of the emotions to get to that light. She helped me talk through all of my emotions:

The sadness because he was gone.

The man who had been a constant in my life for over 25 years.

The man who was my children's father and loved me the best he knew how.

My Tunnel of Grief

On the other hand, I felt a strong sense of relief:

Relief from years of being on my guard because of the negative side of Eric—the side I couldn't live with…the reason for the divorce…the side that hurt me mentally, emotionally, and financially…the side that made me question my own sanity at times. It was a relief to finally not have to worry about what he would do next to mess up our lives. I was angry that he left me to raise the boys alone.

Acknowledging those emotions was the first step in my healing.

I decided to stop drinking and start talking—talking to my counselor and, more importantly, talking to God. God kept reminding me that I was stronger than I thought. Each day, I started believing it more and more. I listened to positive audio books. They helped me uncover my hope and reminded me that I had been through worse. I was resilient. I started coming out of the tunnel.

As I started paying closer attention to my children, I could see that they were hurting just as much. We started talking to each other and sharing and praying together. We made an agreement to share when we were sad or missing him. Each day got better.

Setbacks came, such as when my oldest had an anxiety attack at school. He had been trying to be strong for me and he needed help for himself. My youngest started having problems at school. I realized that we **ALL** needed special support. So, both my boys got counselors to meet their needs. I realized that I had to also support them in areas that their dad had, like scouts and sports.

I also took time away for myself. My first solo vacation to Punta Cana, I remember walking to the beach and stepping into the water. I felt like something just pulled the sadness from me and out into the water. It was released. I won't say I didn't feel sadness ever again; however, it wasn't the heavy all-draining sadness of grief.

I remember talking to someone else who was grieving and sharing how I felt. It helped them. I think that was the point that I realized I was close to the end of the tunnel. I was no longer keeping it inside; rather, I was sharing it as a testimony.

Our lives changed. My life changed. I went from every other weekend to myself, to a full-time single mom of two

My Tunnel of Grief

active boys. I've become a 'sports mom'. I have released some of my activities but gained new ones. Although I had to learn to ask for help (because I couldn't do it all alone), these changes were good. There was new light and energy in our lives!

I ask myself, "*When did I come out of the tunnel?*" I would say it was the one-year anniversary of Eric's passing. I cried but they were different tears. It was sadness because Eric wouldn't see all of the wonderful things that would happen in our lives. I was, however, thankful for the love he did give. I choose to remember the good things.

Through this experience, God told me I had a message to share and a heart to support others. Just because Eric's time was over, that didn't mean **MY** time was over.

In April 2017, my blog and podcast was born to inspire others to greatness and to encourage others to pick up the pieces and move forward. As I reflect back over my life, I have many valleys *AND* victories. I know that I would never have survived without God.

Felicia C. Lucas

"Because of the tender mercy of our God, by which the rising sun will come to us from Heaven to shine on those living in darkness and in the shadow of death, to guide our feet into the path of peace."

Luke 1:78-79

The Two Journeys

The Two Journeys
By: Elder Lorrie Crawley

Seems like just yesterday, she was born: Kitara Janay Crawley. She was born on September 29, 1987 at Duke University at 9:00 a.m. She was delivered by C-section and was taken immediately to PIC-U. I was told that when I came from under anesthesia, she would most likely be dead — but Kitara **survived**! Kitara was born with several life-threatening health issues: transposition of the great vessels, one functioning kidney, cerebral palsy, and an encephalocele. Given no expectancy to live, **SHE LIVED!**

It was time to take Kitara home and we were told that the best thing for her would be to place her in a facility where she could die. My husband and I talked with my family, and my dad told me that she was our child. If we wanted to bring her, then bring her home. We did. We both were unsure of how to take care of her but everything we needed to know came naturally. There was a period when I grieved about not having what we call a "perfect, normal child". I also had to deal with the guilt of her condition being my fault.

I questioned God. *Why did this happen to us? What did we do to have our child be born like this? Why was He punishing us?* I was always told that God knows what He is doing and that I should not question Him; however, I wanted and needed answers.

When I looked at my little girl lying there with so much life and love, I pushed aside my grief, sorrow, and self-pity and came to understand that Kitara was designed for a purpose from the beginning and that she was made from love. I had to overcome the guilt that I felt before I could be a parent to Kitara. From a place deep within me, I overcame my guilt and found peace and acceptance. With the journey of acceptance came a support network from family, friends, and professionals.

The mere fact that Kitara had the will to live gave me the strength I needed to become her parent, caregiver, and advocate. I saw in her the determination to live. I now know that this spirit was given to her to cope with everything that would challenge her will to live.

As I look back at Kitara's life, I understand that it was my faith in God, the support of my family, and the professional resources that we were exposed to helped us to give Kitara the best life possible. Kitara deserved to have the best mom in the world, so that is who I became. During her 14 years on this Earth, she taught me so much. I learned that my happiness and

The Two Journeys

joy were not contingent on having a perfect body; she didn't. Kitara taught me unconditional love because she loved everyone she met. She taught me about patience and so much more. That little, imperfect child was my greatest teacher. She enjoyed life in the "Earth suit" that was designed for her.

Kitara's journey ended on August 28, 2001. She left her mark on this world — a lasting heart of love.

My Journey

Kitara's journey had ended on this Earth and she had begun to experience her new journey back to the Father. Little did I know: I was about to embark on my own journey.

It was in that same year — 2001 — I received some devastating news from my doctor: I had Breast Cancer! Wow! *How could this be happening to me? I just buried my only little girl. I was still going through the grieving period!*

As I reflect back, I was angry with God. He didn't heal my baby like I thought He would. I prayed. I fasted. I believed God would heal Kitara and that she would walk; however, I now understand God had a bigger and better plan.

Felicia C. Lucas

One day, as I was asking God "**WHY?**", I heard the Spirit of God say that He loved me, He loved Kitara, He was her Father, and He was my Father. He knew the journey I had to walk out and I wouldn't be able to fight for my life and Kitara's, too. It was during this time I began to learn God in a unique way. I knew Him as **GOD**; now I was going to understand Him as *FATHER*.

The first journey through Breast Cancer took me to a place I had never been before. There were so many emotions that filled my mind but fear was the root cause of all my emotions.

I was afraid that I would die.

I was afraid that I would have to leave my boys here to be raised by their dad all alone.

I was afraid of the surgery.

I was afraid of the treatment I was going to have to take.

One day while in prayer, I heard my Father say to me that I was not a "victim"; I was a **VICTOR**! That was my stance and that's what I would say to anyone who asked how I was doing. This became my mantra! I said it to my doctors and anyone else who would hear me. I refused to give up. The will

The Two Journeys

to live became like a wellspring in my soul, bubbling into everlasting life! This was my first battle with Cancer.

In the Spring of 2003, the same monster reared its ugly head again. This time, I was not easily-shaken. I was a little more grounded. Don't get me wrong: It wasn't like I wanted this to happen to me again but this time, I was ready for the fight. Once again, my mantra was that I was not a "victim"; I was a **VICTOR**! I would *LIVE* and not die.

The only difference between the first Cancer experience and this one was that this time, they would have to take my breast. I hated losing my hair again but I could handle that. This time, they were going to take a part of me that I felt made me a woman. Questions began to crowd my mind like:

Would my husband still find me desirable?

Would I be less of a woman?

How would this affect my marriage and sex-life?

After the mastectomy, I became depressed. One night, my husband told me something that would send that spirit back to Hell from where it came. He told me that he didn't marry me for my breast but that he loved me. **THAT'S** why he married me. I realized then that I was a beautiful woman with or without breasts!

Let's fast-forward to 2013. It was October and my family was dealing with the death of my mother who had transitioned to her Heavenly Home in July of that year. This experience was so very hard. I felt like a child lost in a mall or park looking for my mother but couldn't find her. I knew where my mother was; however, the pain of not having her here with me was just too much to bear.

My siblings and I depended upon each other to make sense of the whole matter. We had done all the right things that we knew to do to see our mom made whole again. We surrounded her with prayer, gospel music, and the Word of God—24 hours a day. We even changed her diet to a plant-based one. Still, none of that kept her from sleeping away. It was only four years later when we all came to know that we had to submit to both the Father's and my mother's sovereign will for her to return to her Father.

It was during that time—October 2013—that I was told for the third time that the giant called 'Cancer' was back yet again! Well, I had about all that I could take of this and I knew I was in the fight for my very life!

The Two Journeys

I told my siblings and other family members that I needed them to not be afraid, to think what I thought, and to say only what I said. What I said was what **GOD** said about me, which was:

"I will live and not die, to declare the glory of GOD!"

I went into this fight with the iron will that I learned from Kitara. I made a vow to myself and my Father that after this battle was over, I would be a spokesperson for women who would go through the journey of Breast Cancer and that I would be an encourager to women to have an intimate relationship with God as "Abba", Daddy-God.

During the treatment, I received a word from my former Pastor that this time, the head of the giant called 'Cancer' was cut off in my life like David cut off the head of Goliath!

I am a VICTOR! I am a SURVIVOR!

Felicia C. Lucas

"Whoever dwells in the shelter of the Most High will rest in the shadow of the Almighty.
I will say of the LORD,
"He is my refuge and my fortress, my God, in whom I trust."

Psalm 91:1-2

Bouncing Back After a Personal Loss (Resource Chapter)
By: Vernessa Blackwell

We all know what it's like to be in a relationship with someone we love. It can be a first love, one of many, or a long-term relationship such as a marriage. The feelings we share change our lives and fill us with a profound sense of joy. Then one day, something changes and the partner decides to follow a different path. Suddenly, we find ourselves alone. In these cases, it seems that finding joy is a difficult task — but it doesn't have to be that way. The extra-substantial the loss, the greater excessive the grief; however, even subtle losses can cause grief. As an instance: You would possibly experience grief after transferring away from home, graduating from college, converting jobs, selling your circle of domestic relatives, or retiring from a profession you loved.

What is Grief?

Grief is a natural reaction to loss. It's the emotional suffering you sense when something or someone you like is taken away. The more sizeable the loss, the more intense the grief will be. You could associate grief with the loss of life of a loved-one (which is often the purpose of the maximum severe kind of grief) but any loss can purpose grief, consisting of:

- Divorce or relationship break-up
- Loss of financial stability
- Loss of a cherished dream
- Selling the family home
- A miscarriage
- Loss of health
- Losing a job
- Retirement
- Death of a pet
- A loved-one's serious illness
- Loss of a friendship
- Loss of safety after a trauma

Everyone Grieves Differently

Grieving is a personal and notable character. The way in which you grieve depends on many factors which include your character, coping fashion, life experience, religion, and the nature of the loss. Grieving takes time. Recuperation occurs regularly; it can't be forced or moved quickly. There is no "regular" timetable for grieving. A few humans start to sense better in weeks or months. For others, the grieving method is measured in years. Something your grief enjoys is that it is essential to be patient with yourself and allow the system to clearly spread.

Bouncing Back After a Personal Loss

How to Find Joy After a Personal Loss

A lot of people are looking for ways to find true happiness after the loss of their loved-one. At any given moment, people are constantly seeking out those things that will bring them pleasure and make life worth living. Fortunately, happiness is not that hard to find. By utilizing the Law of Attraction, a satisfactory life experience can be obtained almost instantly.

Tell Your Story

One of the most powerful ways to heal from grief is to bring your feelings, emotions, and thoughts to the surface. Sharing your grief experience can be healing. Writing your innermost thoughts that you can go back to and remind you of what you feel and desire can be uplifting. If you are not keeping a journal or diary, begin today. It is strongly recommended you begin a "Grief Relief Journal" or diary. There is great empowerment in expressing your sorrow. This is to be for your own use so that you can write your thoughts and feelings down with no need to filter or edit what is going on inside your mind or heart. Start **TODAY**!

Felicia C. Lucas

Grief Never Finishes

Because of a dreadful, sorrowful condition, your life changed. Only when you understand what grief is and how powerfully it can imprison your thoughts, emotions, and even your whole persona, can you begin to work through your grief. Grieving is a passageway of time; not a place to stay. Nonetheless, grief is not ever completely cured or entirely healed. Mourning may continue. Reconciliation of your sorrowful condition brings into harmony the grieving you experience. This leads to healing. Seize all of the moments of every day to overcome loss, grief, and sorrow.

Grief is the Price of Living Through Life's Circumstances

When your grief-happening encompassed you, your life was most likely altered permanently. Grief is not a lack of faith nor a sign of weakness. What you do with your grief is your choice alone. Understanding your grief and what you can do about healing helps you begin your healing journey to a healthier, happier place in life. Make a list of five steps you must take to understand and reconcile your complex grief. Begin following them **TODAY**!

Bouncing Back After a Personal Loss

Re-Evaluate Your Outlook

You may have to evaluate what has changed and explore what is still possible for you after a life-altering occurrence. It may take some time and patience for you to find your equilibrium again. Begin by recognizing that some of the shifts which have occurred in your life as a result of your experiences are likely to be permanent. List at least three actions you can take in the next week that will propel you forward towards greater happiness. Consider the possibility that your new path will be revealed as you progress. Courageously continue your journey while embracing the hope of greater understanding, peace, and joy to come.

Find a Grief Partner

Trying to survive your grief without the help of others to give comfort and support is not a good option. Trying to overcome your sorrow alone will hinder your progress and may even cause you to become severely depressed due to loneliness and isolation. It is essential that you seek support from others and find ways to express your needs. A partner relationship is essential to your well-being and happiness. Sometimes, all you need to do is ASK: "*I need you to spend time with me and here are my needs...*" Cry with someone. At times, it can be more healing than crying alone. Great comfort and peace—even hope—can come to those who know they have someone to whom they can turn to in time of crisis or need.

Embrace Each Positive Moment

In doing so, you can better find healing, harmony, hope, peace, and joy in living. Peace and joy go together. While it is necessary to pass through the grieving process, don't allow grief to take away your faith in God, love of life, and, most importantly, your hope. Don't be sluggish; be proactive each day in seeking every hopeful and beneficial moment of each possibility for inner-peace.

Turn Inward and Be Compassionate

Right now, discovering how to turn inward and be compassionate with yourself is perhaps one of your most important needs. Embracing your feelings of loss is essential to your survival and future happiness. The grief from a life-altering circumstance may never go away completely. Learning how to reconcile your life after a time of loss requires self-nurturing and self-love to enable you to move through your grief.

Bouncing Back After a Personal Loss

Reconnect with Your Passions

Because of the agony and heartache, you may have temporarily withdrawn from people, places, or things that you previously enjoyed. While a temporary hiatus may be necessary for your healing process, isolation is not a healthy nor beneficial long-term strategy. In your "Grief Relief Journal", jot down the people, places, and things that have brought you the most joy and satisfaction in your life. Ask yourself how many of them can still be a part of your life now. Consider how long it has been since you have engaged with them. Make a plan. Schedule some time each day to involve yourself in something or with someone you have previously enjoyed. Give yourself the gift of something to look forward to each day. Have faith and hope, and contentment will return.

Practice Mindfulness

Mindfulness is cognizance of the present moment with reputation and without judgment. The tendency of thoughts is to decide our revel as excellent or unsightly, good or horrific, and then we strive to keep away from or numb out the stories that we choose as ugly, including grief. We can't selectively numb our pain without also numbing tremendous emotions, like pleasure. See if you could permit the feelings of grief to be and actually note them with compassion. When we are able to open our hearts to our struggling, we will start to thaw out the emotional numbness, which makes room for us to begin to open to greater joy.

Exercise Mindful Self-Care

Consume healthily, get adequate sleep, and exercise your frame. Get out into nature, breathe fresh air, and take in the splendor of the natural with your senses. Try cultivating an awareness (perhaps a gentle yoga practice). Agenda time for 'being' instead of your usual 'doing'.

Write About the Loss

Writing may be therapeutic. Try writing approximately what happened and the way you sense it for about 20 minutes. If it feels right, try repeating the practice four times this week; however, if it feels overwhelming, do something that feels soothing, like consuming a warm cup of tea, taking a warm bath, going for a walk, or taking note of a soothing song. Attempt to write once more later, just in case you sense up to it. Research shows that although this exercise may bring up unpleasant feelings of unhappiness, it could have wonderful long-term results for your health and well-being.

Bouncing Back After a Personal Loss

Have Fun with Easy Pleasures

Take time to experience something satisfying with your senses, like looking at a lovely flower or inhaling its perfume, noticing the splendid blue sky, being attentive to the morning birdsong, taking part in something beautiful in nature, or taking note of nature's song. If it seems like you can't find delight in these types of everyday things, strive to find something simple, like playing with the feel of cold water in your mouth or warm water on your pores and skin inside the shower or bath. Take a few moments to savor the experience and the way in which you sense with your body, heart, and mind. Then, bear in mind the experienced numerous instances all throughout the day.

Make Meaning from the Loss

Try to find some meaning within the loss with the aid of identifying methods that has helped you grow or ended up more resilient to the strain or loss. When you have moved from the depths of grief and are nicely on your way towards the direction of recovery, discover how you can embrace the loss fully to facilitate recuperation through others and your surroundings.

Exercise Pleasure

Similar to being a gift with the grief, it's equally critical to practice beginning joy. Make time to do things that you love and give yourself permission to sense again.

Live Well

Loss reminds us that existence is short. Use times of loss as a possibility to think again about your own life and start to invite questions to yourself about whether you are living a lifestyle full of joy, doing what you adore, and make meaning in your life. Begin to live deliberately, consciously choosing how you live your life. View this as a risk to steadily make some adjustments that can help you live mindfully — and work to stay that way!

Adjust Your Attitude

Assuming things are worse than they've ever been before, it may be difficult to find a reason to smile. Why should you be happy with the way things are if everything's wrong and nothing is going your way? According to the Law of Attraction, like attracts like. For example: If you're upset, you're going to attract more upsetting energies into your life. Have you ever noticed that when you're having a bad day, nothing seems to go right? Instead, what happens is that everyone and everything ends up getting in your way. What most people do not realize is that it is their attitudes that attract worse situations **AND** individuals into their lives. By adjusting your attitude, you'll begin to attract more positive people and circumstances into your life.

Count Your Blessings

If you really want to know how to find true happiness, focus on what you already have going for you. Do you have a place to call 'home'? If so, that's much more than a lot of people have. You might also have a spouse, girlfriend/boyfriend, job, vehicle, children, and great friends. Any one of these things is a lot more than many individuals currently have. Think about those less fortunate. Also, imagine your life without what you have currently and suddenly, you will realize just how truly blessed you already are!

Pay Attention to the Small Things that Make You Happy

Focusing on the small things is an effective way to draw positive energy into your life. Any source of happiness — such as your daily walk to the mailbox, your 30 minutes of "me-time" early in the morning before everyone else wakes up, your cup of coffee, your daily 20-minute walk outside, etc. — is going to help multiply your feelings of joy, attracting more true happiness into your life. When you're busy enjoying those small, daily, and simple pleasures, make sure that you really soak up the feelings of pleasure that you experience. Notice how that joy leaks over into other areas of your life.

Turn Negatives into Positives

Realizing that you don't have control over everything that happens in your life is very important. Knowing how to find true happiness won't be possible until you can learn how to turn all of the negatives in your life into positives. It may be difficult to derive something positive from every situation but if you look carefully enough, you will find something positive in everything!

Practice Makes Perfect

Remember to begin with the simple things in life. As you begin to experience more pleasure by enjoying the small things, you will notice that your life begins to change drastically. Suddenly, more people will want to be around you, you'll be presented with more opportunities, and you'll find that your life is working out much better than you had ever imagined possible.

Bouncing Back After a Personal Loss

Life unavoidably includes experiencing loss; however, loss ought not result in hopelessness. If we take the time to expand a non-secular route that prepares us to domesticate the heart to be present to whatever arises, we are able to start to increase a feeling of internal refuge that prepares us to satisfy whatever life brings our way. While we learn to balance being a gift with our grief with an opening to joy, we find 'wish'. We may additionally even discover that commencing our hearts to our grief and joy results in experiencing a sense of more aliveness and joy than we were able to access previous to the loss!

Seize the Flower Petals of Renewal and Rebirth — TODAY!

Renewal and rebirth begin and end with you. Start now. How you do it is a personal matter but is vital to finding happiness, new peace, and joy. Also, seek God's help to give additional inspiration, strength, and wisdom to carry your grief cross. Consider saying a silent prayer. If you are out of practice, it is okay; you will feel additional comfort and peace when you continue to let humble thoughts flow. The more you do so with consistency and sincere effort, the great the possibility for inspiration from God. Ponder deeply all the steps you might take to renew hope and find rebirth in a fuller life.

Count Your Grateful Moments

Be specific. Some blessings will be big and some small. They all count! As you count your blessings, you will be surprised at how many things you feel gratitude about. Count the blessings one by one. Realizing what you are grateful for will give you strength in times of discouragement. Acting upon your intentions to be grateful can bring you rich blessings. Practice gratitude every day to foster gratefulness in your life. Write at least five things in your journal that you are grateful for today.

You Are NOT Alone

Because of your deep sorrow, it can be extremely difficult for you to believe (in this moment) that there can be hope, joy, and peace in your life. If you are going through a time of grief in your life, recognize that while your journey of grief is unique, you can take comfort in the hope and wisdom from those who have walked the path of grief before you. Can you let literally thousands of others who grieved before you give you hope? You are **NOT** alone. Think of three ways of how others have been able to reconcile their grief. Consider searching the Internet for stories of how others have met their difficult challenges successfully. Let those examples empower you!

Bouncing Back After a Personal Loss

Gather Precious Moments

Seek to enjoy life and its gifts. Recognize the value of living in the moment. Believe in possibilities beyond what you may see today. You are invited to pluck each day's happenings as if you were gather precious moments like flowers. Are you? Experiment with ideas and actions to find the ones that resonate the most with you and support your healing. Taking actions on new ideas and concepts can help you find new purpose and understanding. Find the solutions that can support your healing. Take action today and always.

If you want to have a better life, you have to make sure certain things are included in your life more often to help ensure you get the life you want. One of these things you must make sure to have presented as often as possible is ***JOY***! Joy is central to so many other things. Joy can lead to happiness. Joy can lead to smiling and laughing. Joy leads to so many positive and wonderful things. The key is to do four things on a regular basis in order to have as much joy as possible in your life.

What Brings YOU Joy?

You must begin by having a clear understanding of what joy feels like to you and what helps bring joy into your life. If we want to have more joy in our lives, it is logical that we understand what it is and how we can get it. Each of us finds joy in different things. For example, I find joy in sending simple "thinking of you" Skype messages to my friends and seeing their reactions. I enjoy giving a hug to someone who seems stressed — if for no other reason than to break the funk they are in. You must find what brings you joy so you can experience that feeling more often.

Celebrate Your Moments of Joy

This may seem a little silly since joy is already something of a celebratory thing; however, this is an important step towards having more joy in your life. When we celebrate things that we want in our lives, we open ourselves up to receiving these things more often. So, when you celebrate your moments of joy, you are asking for more of those moments of joy to come into your life. Don't just note, "*Wow! That was a nice moment of joy!*" Really **CELEBRATE**! Get up and dance! Tell someone else about it! Do whatever you have to do in order to **TRULY** celebrate it!

Celebrate the Moments of Joy of Others

This is building upon the lessons from the previous section. When you learn to celebrate your own joy, you bring more of it to you. The same is true for others when you help

Bouncing Back After a Personal Loss

them celebrate their moments of joy. This is a huge thing, a big deal, and something that will take some getting used to. Sadly, people are not used to celebrating good things that happen to them. This may end up making them uncomfortable at first. That is okay; just explain why you want to celebrate it and the benefits of doing the celebration. It will pay off in the long run if you do it. Make them feel safe and comfortable. Perhaps make the initial celebration more low-key. This will help them and also help you by teaching you more ways to celebrate and experience joy.

Choose Joy

The final word on all of this 'joy stuff' is simple: Joy is a state of mind that we either choose to be in or exclude ourselves from. Ultimately, the state of joy is a choice you get to make. If it makes you feel good, makes you happier, makes your life better, and makes the lives of those around you better, why wouldn't you choose joy? It may take you a little time to learn to choose joy, so if you follow the other techniques discussed in this chapter, you will get better at this *'JOY THING'* and it will come more naturally for you.

So, **CHOOSE JOY**! It really can be *THAT* simple!

"Surely, He hath borne our griefs and carried our sorrows."

Isaiah 53:4a

Against ALL Odds
By: Malissa Stringer

It is so amazing that you can go through so many tests and trials, yet not look like what you've been through. We all have a story to tell. This is how mine begins:

- I was born a preemie.
- I was molested between the ages of 3 to 11.
- Because of the molestation, I was sexually active at an early age.
- Being the youngest of five children, I was given up to another family.
- My brother was brutally murdered when I was 12 years old.
- I got pregnant for the first time at 17 years old.
- I was almost killed by an ex-boyfriend who was riding along with my child and I in the car. He attempted to crash us all into the police station by putting his foot on the gas pedal — but GOD blocked it!
- In my life, I've dealt with a lot of rejection.
- After finishing my Master's degree at age 37, I was diagnosed with Breast Cancer.

Felicia C. Lucas

As you can see, the title of this book is called *The Bounce Back*. God has given me the ability to get my 'bounce back' in spite of all that I've gone through. Although none of what I went through was easy to experience, I understand the purpose of me going through those things was to be able to help someone else trying to get their bounce back: the person reading this book…**YOU**!

Many times, when we are living through the lesson that we will someday reflect back upon, it is extremely difficult to understand why we have to go through them at that time. Fast-forward to the present, where hopefully with age comes the understanding that every challenge life presented was a teachable moment.

There was a time in my life when I would pray every day that God would allow me to be a living testimony. At the time I was saying that prayer, I never knew what I was asking of God—that was until the diagnosis of Cancer came up. One question that is not uncommon for Cancer patients is: "*Why did this happen to* **ME**?" That was a question I **never** asked because I knew that God knows all. He did not make any mistakes and it was all a part of His divine plan for my life. It took me about two years following the initial diagnosis to understand that

Against ALL Odds

God allowed Cancer to happen to change my life so that I could change the lives of others.

Since the diagnosis, I was fired from my job in Corporate America. That firing was one of the best things that could have ever happened to me. After getting fired, I was able to move into my passion full time: To inspire others to be the best that they can be!

To my surprise, I began working as a substitute teacher. As a substitute, I began to speak to the children on a daily basis about the importance of self-love, self-respect, and self-acceptance — things that we, as adults, have a lot to learn about. I would ask the children, *"Who are you?"* That's a question I would also ask adults during my conferences because I began to see that so many people did not know who they were. Their responses always amazed me. We have so many distractions in our lives that take us away from getting to know ourselves, especially during an age where we are inundated with technology. The noise in our lives can keep us from realizing our worth (when I say 'noise', please understand that I am referring to the people in our lives whom we've allowed to speak negatively into our spirits, negativity of the songs and television shows we listen to/watch, all of the facades of social media that allow us to hide who we truly are, etc.). The list of 'noise' could go on and on.

This is a great place for reflection. I want you to take this time to understand that you are priceless. I want you to understand that you are not reading these words by chance. It is my desire to help you understand that you are valuable royalty, awesome, brilliant, and authentic because you are uniquely and wonderfully made. God created you to be a masterpiece. There is none like you—nor will there ever be.

I'm sure that like me, you have been through some things. As I said in the beginning, we all have our own story. Maybe your start has not been as difficult as mine…or perhaps it was worse. Wherever you may be in your journey, don't be moved by what you see. Believe that your best days are yet to come. Understand the power of your words and be careful about those things you speak over your life—meaning when you say things about yourself, they become magnets and attach themselves to you. As a result, when you do speak over your life, be **INTENTIONAL** about it. Speak **LIFE** into ever situation that you deal with. Anticipate the challenges of life. Know that adversity will come; therefore, stay in a constant state of readiness. Never forget that there is not testimony without the 'test'.

Against ALL Odds

Earlier, I began this chapter with many of the things I had experienced in my life. Although those things were difficult for me to go through—and even more difficult to express—it has brought me to a place of healing through sharing my experiences. I understand that the things I've been through shaped me to be the person I am today. If I could do it all over again, I don't know that I would change anything. Through my pain, I have been able to change the lives and perspectives of those around me. There are some things you can't put a price on; however, being able to look people in the eye and honestly be able to tell them, *"I've been there"*, is therapeutic for both of us.

Because of the very things that I have gone through, I've been allowed to be thrusted into my destiny. I am now an Author and Motivational Speaker. I am confidently walking in my passion. Speaking life into someone else gives me life as I help people discover their worth and teach them to run after their dreams. That is what I truly live for. I am so glad God saw that my life was worth saving for a time such as this!

I am not going to sit here and tell you that the path was always easy; nor will I sit here and tell you that there weren't times when I thought about giving up. I will, however, tell you that giving up would have been the **WORST** decision I would have ever made, especially when there were so many opportunities to give up. I am thankful that I made the decision to turn obstacles into opportunities.

People often consider giving up because it feels easier than going through whatever the issue is at hand. That might actually be true…to a degree. I can assure you that the reward is so much greater when you know that you have hung in there and fought to the bitter end. Furthermore, be encouraged that perseverance pays off. No matter what you're facing, even though you may not understand it right now, there will come a time in your life when you will look back and have an "AH-HA! Moment". It would be during this time that you will see **ALL** things have worked together for your good.

Before I close, I would like to leave you with some food for thought:

- Take risks often because as the old saying goes, "Without risk, there is no reward".
- Build your legacy like a building: one brick at a time.
- Times will be tough but enjoy the journey on your way to success.
- Be confident about your worth; never settle for anything less than you deserve.

Against ALL Odds

- Fear nothing because it's nothing more than '**F**alse **E**vidence **A**ppearing **R**eal'. Everything that you go through is relational according to your perspective. Learn to view things through a different lens.
- "Obstacles in life are like traffic jams; they eventually clear."

Move forward, stay the course, be obedient to your calling, and get your **BOUNCE BACK**! God did it for me; there is no question He will do it for you! Check out Romans 2:11!

Felicia C. Lucas

"He heals the brokenhearted and binds up their wounds."

Psalm 147:3

Forgiveness Led Me to Love
By: Louvanta White

Hello to all of the beautiful gems who will be reading this chapter! This is a very touching chapter. In no way is this written to display any forms of hatred, dislike, or demoralize any human being. My intentions are to help others heal, forgive, and enjoy the beautifulness of **LOVE**. As you explore this chapter, I hope you take something from it and share with others. Thank you so much for your support. Much love to you all!

Ms. Beautiful Gem Louvanta

****

Have you ever experienced something that had you questioning, *"Why* **ME***?"* or *"What could I have done to deserve* **THIS***?"* Have you ever felt like you wanted to die because of a dark secret that lived inside of you? Well, My Gems: I, too, have felt this way. I experienced something that I wouldn't wish on anyone—not even my worst enemy. What I'm about to share with you is something that most people are afraid to speak on. Some people like to shove this topic away. **NOT I!** Although this topic affected my life, it didn't take me out of the game. I truly thank God for healing, love, grace, and mercy!

Felicia C. Lucas

Let's explore how I **BOUNCED BACK** from sexual abuse...

I was born and raised on the West side of Chicago (Austin area). I am the oldest of eight siblings. I come from a very strong family. Growing up as a child, I didn't want for anything. My mom made sure all of our needs were met. As a child, I enjoyed doing a lot of things like playing with my dolls, video games, jumping rope, climbing trees, football, etc. Although those things made me happy, I was living with this dark secret that I was ashamed of and didn't know how to speak on because I was so afraid. I was four years old when my innocence was taken. I remember that horrific night like no other...

I was sitting in the living room area. We were watching TV and this individual began asking me questions. I didn't know what anything meant. **I was FOUR!** I was advanced to be four years old but still...I was a *CHILD*. You see, he was very abusive and had a way with his words. This individual used intimidation to instill fear in me.

Going back to the night he placed his hand in my shirt... I asked him to stop. I was feeling uncomfortable. He told me to **"Shut up"**. I pleaded with him, *"Please stop. This doesn't feel*

Forgiveness Led Me to Love

good". Someone was coming upstairs and the violation stopped. I thought I was safe and that it wouldn't happen again. I was wrong. The next time he got me, it was the full force. He reminded me about the first encounter, slapped me, and hit me in the back of my head. All I could remember were the words: *"This is your fault. You made me do this to you."*

This went on for years. When I turned seven, I finally fought back. I put a knife to his throat and told him if he ever touched me again, I was going to kill him. Of course, he thought I was crazy — but the abuse stopped.

Although that was over, I still wrestled with the emotional aftermath of the abuse. I couldn't sleep at night. I had no respect for men. I developed a drinking habit to cope with the hurt. I made poor relationship decisions, etc., etc., etc.

Later in my life, I found Jesus. All of that hurt, guilt, and shame I had to let go. I later faced my abuser and told him I forgave him for what he did to me. He said he couldn't even remember what I was talking about. It was okay, though. I felt great forgiving him so that I could properly heal.

In order for us to heal from our past experiences, we have to forgive one another and, sometimes, even ourselves.

When it comes to sexual abuse, you can't just "get over it"; however, with **GOD** on your side, the healing process becomes easier.

What helped me was knowing that God forgives me for every sin I commit. Who am I to condemn another? I have no Heaven or Hell to put anyone in. All I can do is pray for them.

In conclusion, I want to leave you with some tips on forgiveness. I want you to find it in your heart to make peace with the parties involved (or perhaps yourself):

- Identify the problem or situation.
- Pray for the individuals and yourself.
- Reconcile or reconnect with the individuals who caused you hurt or pain.
- Allow the healing process to begin. Take it one day at a time.
- Let go and let **GOD**!

I hope this chapter blessed you. I hope these tips bless you. I challenge you to forgive those who may have hurt you. Get your peace, happiness, and joy! Get *YOURSELF* back! Take care!

Forgiveness Led Me to Love

"For if you forgive other people when they sin against you, your Heavenly Father will also forgive you. But if you do not forgive others their sins, your Father will not forgive your sins."

Matthew 6:14-15

Felicia C. Lucas

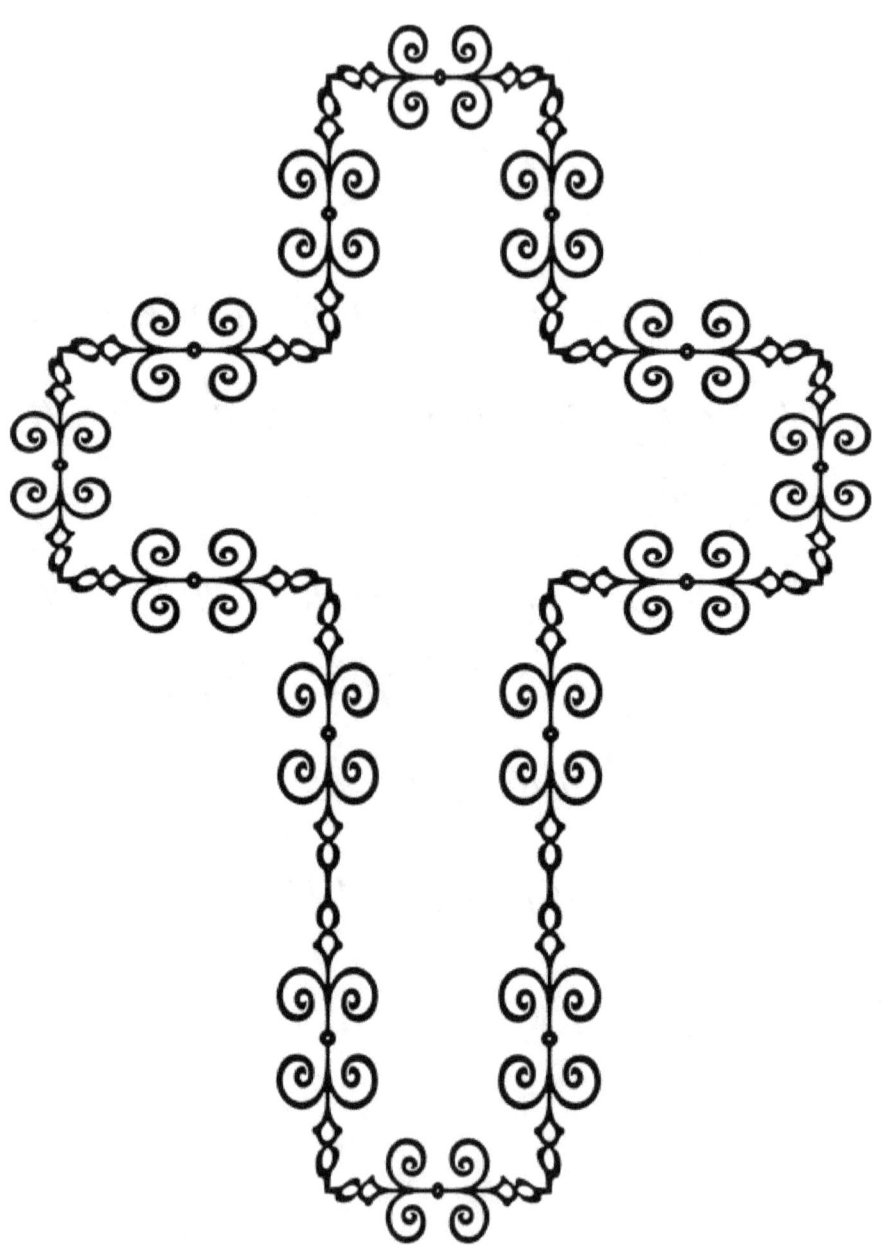

I Am a Striver, Believer, and Conqueror!

I am a Striver, Believer, and Conqueror!
Blessed, Determined, and Humble
By: DuWanda S. Epps

For beginners, I tested the waters of so-called 'love' early on in life. My first serious relationship began at the age of 13. Knowing nothing about genuine love, I was too young to mentally comprehend that love shouldn't hurt. Growing up in a household that seemed to argue and fight on a regular basis was my example of love. It was very frightening, especially for a child who can remember graphic images of blood shed by my mother from fist fights with my dad. I was around four years old then. The sounds of her frightening cries would make any human shiver.

Young and naïve, I didn't have a healthy relationship role model outside of the dream families you would find on television. My childhood was basically in the projects of the South Bronx and life in Harlem, New York. Hustlers of all kinds, drug addicts, and alcoholics were everywhere. My pops was well-known in the streets and my mom was all over the place as she battled the drug demon; however, I always respected my mom and loved her, regardless of what addiction she had. The pillars of strength in our family were the grandmothers on both sides. These women walked with their heads high. They walked with strides of confidence and grace. They were 'Jacks of Trades' and business-oriented (with a minimal education) — but they were no fools to holding down their own.

I was independent from a young age, taking care of my sisters making sure they were good and well-behaved. I experienced dysfunction at the age of 15. The physical and verbal abuse began. I had several major things that took place in my life between the ages of 15 and 18.

At the age of 17 (I was a junior in high school), I became homeless. Shortly after, I found out I was pregnant. I was lost and confused, seeking employment daily with good leads. One thing remained: I always had faith. I found myself sleeping on sofas or making a bed on someone's floor, surviving by eating food from WIC (the government's Women, Infants, and Children program) daily. Months before my baby was born, I returned back home to my grandmother. I went to school, determined to graduate high school. I worked security in addition to working on my studies. I was determined! I was a proud mother and wanted to be able to provide for my daughter, teach her, and be her first positive role model.

I Am a Striver, Believer, and Conqueror!

I continued to love and create a life with my first love since we had a child together. I remained loyal to my fiancé, even through the abuse. I dealt with him and the abuse for over five years. Well, two more awesome, unique children later and completing my Master's degree at the age of 25, it was time to create a better, productive way of living. My children and I relocated to North Carolina—a state I visited only a few times previously. I found a house and had employment lined up in addition to starting my business. I found myself in a new relationship that had both beautiful and dark moments but ultimately ended with my partner being sentenced to 52 months in federal prison.

My children's father reentered our lives but this time around, I had grown up. I was not the same young, naïve girl from years ago. Things between us were bittersweet and ended with a quick twist. When I said, "*I do*", I didn't think about myself. I thought about my children having their father in their lives. I had great thoughts about our family's future but it turned out to be a devastating choice. I entered into a world of deceit, lies, and verbal abuse that quickly spiraled downward.

In the midst, the blessing of working hard day and night afforded me the opportunity to open my behavioral health agency on my birthday in October 2009. We were striving and thriving—until the state enhanced the definitions of Behavioral Health Services. It was too costly to change to the new guidelines as a Small Business Owner. I made the conscious decision to voluntarily terminate my contract with my local management entity. Shortly afterward, I was unemployed and seeking employment yet again.

Newly-married and with bills mounting, I found myself in a state of depression. I didn't want to be married any longer because he was doing more harm than good. I felt broken, lost, and alone trying to sustain my family while my husband was in New York committing acts of adultery. I caught him three times…three times too many. Less than six months into our marriage, I filed for a divorce. I moved my children and I out of our house and into an income-based apartment. I found myself taking several steps backwards in order to move forward.

I felt as if I was being punished by signing a death sentence, agreeing to marry into a union of dysfunction and lies. When I love, I love with all of my heart. I also felt violated and played with in the worst way. It seemed as if he reentered our lives just to attempt to destroy them.

Lost. Alone. Angry. Destroyed. That's how I was left to feel. Once I walked away, I had no thought of marriage, let

I Am a Striver, Believer, and Conqueror!

alone a romantic relationship with another man. I needed time to rebuild and forgive myself—and my husband. The Lord was working on me because the same female who knew my husband was very married yet continued to have sexual relations with him eventually apologized to me and shared her reasons relating to why she pursued the adulterous relationship with my husband. Sister to sister, I found it in my heart to *FORGIVE* all that was done to me. Not long after, **LOVE** that I did not expect (or want at the time) found **ME**! I wasn't afraid to love again; I just didn't *WANT* to. **BUT GOD!** He had a person just for **ME**.

Through all I have experienced in life, **GOD** has always kept me. In darkness, the unknown, the unexpected, the pain, the tears, the lack, and homelessness, *MY LORD KEPT ME!*

I married the one who was made just for me. The song I walked down the aisle to was Maurette Brown Clark's *The One He Kept for Me*. That song describes my life and all of the feelings I felt while going through my storms. The light was bright at the end of my dark tunnel.

Although marriage is not a simple walk in the park, you have to push forward. Every day can be a battle. At times, I

Felicia C. Lucas

want to give up…but I don't. I ask that you not give up, either. I learned to make necessary changes and keep moving forward. When events occur that try to knock you out of the game, use them as lessons in life — and keep moving forward!

I am my past. I am my present. And proudly, I am my future.

I Am a Striver, Believer, and Conqueror!

"I can do all this through Him who gives me strength."

Philippians 4:13

The Girl Who Matured Too Fast
By: Melissa Bridgers-Allen

Your trials and tribulations can hinder or bless you. *Who am I?* The little country farm girl, born and raised in Edgecombe County in an old farm house that sat back about a mile from the highway surrounded by farmland and trees. I am the little girl who loved her little red plastic chair. I am Melissa Bridgers-Allen. Who would have though this little African-American girl who lived in a farm home with my grandparents, mother, and siblings would be successful? Not me! You see, my faith in myself was very weak.

Your past can hinder you. I'm a witness! I am the eldest of two siblings by my mother; therefore, I had a lot of responsibilities. It all started back at the age of three in my grandparents' home where my little red chair sat that my grandfather bought me. You see, I loved my grandparents and they loved me. Everyone always said, "Sweet Thang"—which became my nickname. I was their favorite grandchild and that is where my roots began.

The struggle was real as I watched my grandparents pick cotton, prime tobacco, and raise a farm of pigs, field peas, and corn. We even had a smokehouse where they kept the pork meat. All of what they did was to feed our family. My grandfather would make a fresh pot of coffee every morning. I can still hear him saying, "*Sweet Thang, get your red chair. It's time to eat!*" He would make two cups of coffee: one for him and one for me. Yes: I was three years old drinking coffee. My grandmother would get **so** mad at him because she believed that giving coffee to a child early in life would make that child thick-headed…whatever that meant.

They taught me how to cook, wash clothes, and clean up at an early age. Although they had great values, there was also mental and physical abuse within the home. Alcohol played a huge part in it all. My mother and her siblings would watch my grandfather mentally and physically abuse my grandmother and them as well, which caused my mother and her siblings to soon leave home — and some never looked back.

My mother married my sister's father. We moved in with his mother and family. I always felt like the stepchild because I was treated like one. It got so bad that at the age of seven, my mother told me, "*You're going to stay with your grandparents*". I cried because I didn't want to leave my mother. I knew she was being physically and mentally abused by her husband but at the same time, I was pleased that I was going to live my grandparents whom I loved and I knew loved me. About a

The Girl Who Matured Too Fast

year later, the abuse had gotten so bad, my mother and two sisters moved back in with us at my grandparents' home — and this is where it **ALL** started going downhill.

My mother started drinking heavily **EVERY** day. At the age of nine, we moved to Freedom Hill Apartments in Princeville, North Carolina — a little town next to Tarboro that was founded by freed slaves in 1885. It was there that my maturity kicked in to overdrive. My mother worked a full-time job as a cook which left me home alone with my sisters. Our neighbors watched over us while mom worked. I cooked my first meal at the age of nine. I wanted to help out my mother while she worked, so one day, I cooked a pot of pinto beans and homemade biscuits. My mom was so tickled when she got home. See, back then, we had chores to do around the house to receive an allowance (versus now, children could care less about keeping the house clean or going outside to play).

My father came into town to visit me at the age of 10. I was not looking forward to his visit. All I knew about him was that he took my mother's virginity at the age of 16 and she got pregnant with me. Mom found out he married her sister when my mom was eight months pregnant. That changed her life completely. Therefore, I resented my father for a long time. When he came around, I hated him for hurting my mother. I would say, "*He's not my father. If he died today, I would not care!*" Boy, did my mother get angry when I said that! She sat me down one day and told me that no matter what happened between her and my father, she didn't want to **ever** hear me say those words about him again. It was at that moment I really felt her pain. After all she had been through with him, she still had a loving heart.

Shortly after, my grandmother passed away at the age of 49. Yes, you may say she was young but she lived a rough life. Irish Rose wine was part of her daily routine. She had eight children — the first birthed at the age of 13. My grandfather was much older than her. Soon after grandmother's passing, the family's rituals were destroyed. No more Sunday family dinners or get-togethers. Everyone started drifting their separate ways.

At the age of 12, my life changed again. I lost my virginity to a 16-year-old. You may say I was 'looking for love in all the wrong places'. I was seeking attention. There I was, home alone watching after my sisters while my mother worked. I had no father figure in my life other than my grandfather. I always hung around family and friends older than me. Some would say, "*Girl, you have an old soul!*" I never looked at it that way; I was simply 'seeking'.

The Girl Who Matured Too Fast

In 1991, I lost the closest person to my heart: my grandfather. I felt truly alone at this point. I was 14 years old and so full of hurt because the man who was the "glue" of our family was finally gone. There I stood in the hospital room the evening before he died and watched tears roll down my grandfather's face as I walked into his room. He knew I was going to say my good-byes to him for the last time. Oh, the pain!

Bring on the partying! I started hanging out at night clubs and parties with my older cousins and friends. Mind you: I was only a freshman in high school. I met my first true love a month before my 15th birthday: the man who would be my son's father, "Raymond Best". I can still remember the night we met at a night club. It was love at first sight. Butterflies fluttered in the pit of my belly. Raymond was a senior in high school but that didn't stop us. In April 1992—and one week before my 16th birthday—I found out I was pregnant with our son. I was a sophomore in high school and about to have a baby. During this time, my 12-year-old sister found out she was pregnant as well. My mother had two grandchildren on the way, and they were only nine days apart. Mom's youngest brother was dying from Cancer. A year after that, she lost her father.

Crack Cocaine, meet Mom. Mom, meet Crack Cocaine.

Felicia C. Lucas

After all of the pain my mother endured, she could no longer hold it together. We lost everything. The streets stole our mother; therefore, we had to live with other family members until I turned 18 and got custody of my sisters and niece. Raymond and I moved into a two-bedroom apartment. We both worked to send the younger ones to school and daycare.

On June 9, 1995, my life fell apart. I lost Raymond to an automobile accident. He was only 22 years old. There was a bad storm that day. I can still remember like yesterday asking the State Trooper when he told me the news, *"How do you propose I tell my two-year-old son that his father is never coming home again?"* I fell to my knees, yelling in tears. There I was: lost again. The only person at the time I felt I could depend on to help me with my siblings and who loves us was gone.

It took me five years to wake up from that nightmare. During that time, I wasn't looking for love. I only wanted to party and date different men because in my heart, no one could take Raymond's place and love me the way he did. I found myself asking God often, **"WHY DID YOU TAKE HIM?"**

In 2001, I received my answer when I gave my life to Christ. The answer was so clear. God spoke to me and said, *"It's*

The Girl Who Matured Too Fast

your time". "My time, Lord?" "Yes, my daughter. I want you to use that gift I gave you by helping others."

I started college, took nursing classes full time and worked two jobs. My son and siblings were my inspiration. When I looked at my son, he reminded me so much of his father, so I kept pushing to have a better future for us. I can still remember leaving home while he was asleep and returning when he was asleep after working 16-hour days. It was a struggle…**BUT GOD!** Only He knows all that I endured to get to this point.

Today, I continue to follow the path that God laid before me by being the prudent nurse He designed me to be.

Melissa Bridgers-Allen, R.N.

The success continues. I truly thank God for the trials and tribulations because my struggles made me wiser and stronger. The leash has been broken!

"*Consider it pure joy, my brothers and sisters, whenever you face trials of many kinds, because you know that the testing of your faith produces perseverance.*"

James 1:2-3

Awakened

Awakened
By: Rayshoun Chambers

*A*nd our 2009 Vanguard Award winner is...**Ms. RAYSHOUN CHAMBERS!!!** I could barely feel my legs underneath me. It felt like an eternity getting to the top of the stage. What an out-of-body experience it was being identified as one of the Top Performers in my company!

I often reflect back on that day for mindfulness. You learn so much about things when your recall is honest. When you allow yourself to name the emotions you feel as what they truly are—not what people tell you they should be. The cold, hard truth is this: As I sit here at home tonight looking at the personalized designated parking space sign I had just enjoyed pulling up to so often just a few, short years prior, a flash flood of visions of the weekends and late-night hours of sweat equity keep rushing through my head doing battle with my thoughts and feelings of betrayal, worry, disbelief, and downright "pisstivity". How did this even happen?

The mental playback goes on in my head...

"Rayshoun, when you get a moment, can you come to my office? We're making some changes and I need your assistance with a few things." I could tell by the tone of voice that it was something serious. We always knew within corporate there's a change here or a tweak there; but **THIS** time came across a bit different than other times. So, I waddled my way on down to the breakroom area and prepared my usual 40 ounces of ice water with pieces of fruit before the meeting.

He had the type of office setup where he could see all of the comings and goings of everyone in the parking lot, but people couldn't see inside unless it was night time. I used to "mind-escape" watching people hustle off to lunch and make a beeline back to the office from one of the chairs in there.

"We've been reviewing our financials and we are going to have to make the company leaner. I was hoping you may be able to help me take a look at your staff and let's see how they've been doing. Don't get me wrong: Overall, your areas have been performing very well but do you currently have anyone on the performance plan? Is there anyone you know who just doesn't seem to get the vision? If so, I suggest we start compiling a list so we can get that over to HR and they can see what those separation packages will look like."

It was a long walk back to my desk that day, in part because of the pressure on my pelvis. The day before, my obstetrician advised me that my little one was growing as planned. I smiled so very much during my pregnancy. I truly

Awakened

found something so amazing about the entire process of creating life inside, so I would gleam and glow nearly every day — even through the rough patches of early-onset nausea or having a body temperature be the hottest body temperature in the room. I enjoyed and fully-embraced what it meant to be in the position I was in to be a lady-in-waiting to raise a King.

Now boarding Delta flight number 1672, Phoenix, Arizona. Last boarding call for Delta flight number 1672 — route to Phoenix, Arizona.

I always enjoy the trips out there. The landscaping (in certain aspects) can be really breathtaking but I wasn't going to enjoy all of the fun and frills that come along with such a beautiful environment. I was on my way to *prison*. The thought of heading to Perryville and knowing that I had the opportunity to go exchange information with some of the smartest women I've ever had an opportunity to meet was bittersweet. Choices tend to lead us down a different path. Each time I went there to work with the women, I realized every time there's not much difference between any one of us seated there, other than their choices.

It's funny: I went there to teach information about the electronic payment processing industry, yet each time I left filled with more knowledge and understanding than I came with. They were an awesome team of women.

I can feel the negative emotions slowly melting away thinking back on a conversation with my former boss. He phoned me to let me know I had been commissioned as a Bank Officer and an Assistant Vice President—and I received it on April 1st! I still smile when I think about the conversation I had with him because I truly thought it was an April Fool's Day joke.

The corporate life is fun when done right. So now, a few years later, you can image how overwhelmed I must have felt when I had been asked to attend a meeting with a couple of the executive team suite, advising me the Arizona project was coming to an end. *"We are pulling the plug on the project. We've done some assessments and the project just hasn't turned back the results we need to make this scalable. Slow adoption from the Field Sales Team makes this necessary."* I am watching as one of them slowly turns over an "offer letter" and slides it across the table at me. *"But don't worry. We have a job for you in the company. However, this role does not have an incentive plan or commissions. It's a flat salary."* So, I looked at the two gentlemen and said, "Well, that concerns me deeply. As you know, every single commission plan I have ever had I have exceeded the eight years I've

Awakened

been at this organization. I've been here over eight years, so for me to have the entire commission package removed from any position that I'm working results in a 60% cut in pay for me."

I felt my unborn son moving around in my belly.

One of them said to me, "*Well, you know in your current state, if you don't accept the position, we will have to go ahead and make you a part of the upcoming reorganizational structure/reduction-in-force on next Wednesday. If you quit, your benefits will be ending effective the end of this month and given your current state/condition, you seem to have a little bit further along to go. We truly wish there was something more we can do. I mean, we know it's not the kind of job that requires a lot of skills that you have but we definitely know we could use your help in that area and thought this would be a good option for you*". I didn't know what to feel. At that point, I was unsure if I was feeling anger, fear, or disappointment. I just knew for the first time in many, many years, the reality of need to have more than one stream of income hit me right between the eyes. It was in that very moment, I promised myself and my unborn son that I would **BOUNCE BACK.**

Not long after my son was born, I was contacted by a very longtime friend of mine whose feedback and professional acumen I truly respect. She mentioned to me an opportunity to become a part of a direct-marketing business. I may have been skeptical about my ability to be effective in the business because it was a new type of business but I was not at all skeptical about the fact that I needed an additional revenue stream. I'm so excited about having listened to my inner-self and taking the leap to do what was necessary. I have become a better friend and businesswoman by disregarding my fear of the unknown. I let go of the self-serving pain I was feeling by affixing my personal emotions to business decisions.

When I began to trust in God for the supernatural impossible, the daily pushback of the world became so much smaller to me. The ease of taking struggles and reporting them to my Conqueror, my Provider, my Strength, and my **FATHER** became more of a daily process than a 'Break In Case Of Emergency' type deal I had going on earlier in my spiritual walk. I realized that I am **ENOUGH** with Christ—no matter the location, no matter the role, no matter the territory, no matter the team. That is when things started happening. When I stopped worrying about tomorrow and executing **TODAY**, that is when I began to meet the people who were already on the path to partner with me and change my destiny to be in alignment—not with the things that brought me comfort but with the people, places and things that were destined to help

Awakened

me *GROW*. Above all of this, I can honestly say that it gives me more peace knowing that I am being obedient to the mission I have been called to. By doing that, I am enabling others to do the same.

> "I press on toward the goal to win the prize for which God has called me heavenward in Christ Jesus."
>
> Philippians 3:14

Still Yes!

Still Yes!
By: Pastor Shamielle Alston

Have you ever felt rejected by God? Being rejected by man is one thing, and it brings its own very real pains, struggles, and issues. BUT when you feel that **GOD** has rejected you…when you feel that you're chasing God to no avail, what do you do? Wrestling with this issue sparked a conversation between my best friend and myself:

"Knowing what you now know about life and God, would you get saved again?"

"Hell no!"

"Wow! Seriously? You wouldn't?"

"No. It's too hard!"

My friend was sharp, quick, and precise with her response. She was unapologetically through with God! She had had enough. I wish I could say I was shocked by her response but the mere fact that I posed such a question indicates that I, too, was wrestling with the answer.

If I had to do it all over again, would I? Would I accept Christ as my Savior? Would I vow to live for Him? Would I give Him my all? Would I trust Him with my all? Knowing what I now know about life, would I get saved again? Well…would I?

How did I arrive at such a place? What made me analyze my life in such a manner that it caused me to question the relevance of my life with Christ? There were too many "Whys" without answers.

WHY was I raised in a Foster Home?

WHY do I not have any family?

WHY doesn't anyone love me?

WHY is life so hard?

WHY is everything a struggle?

WHY are there more struggles than successes?

So many "*WHYS*" and not enough answers.

Life is full of responsibilities, expectations, and dreams. The "*WHYS*" of life overshadowed me. I felt as if my responsibilities forbade my expectations, and my expectations laughed at my dreams. Understandably, no one wants to be homeless or an addict but I must admit: there were days when I wished I was an alcoholic or drug addict…or out of my mind. Being one of those would be less painful than being consciously

Still Yes!

aware of the power of God and His sovereignty. That would be less painful than knowing how awesome God is. It would be less painful than realizing we've been given promises by God and watching year after year pass without the promise being released. It would be less painful than knowing the Word of God is alive and standing on that Word; yet not being able to make things work in your life.

After all, is there not scripture after scripture of how God has plans to bless us and not curse us? How we can cast all our cares upon Him? How all things work together for our good? Just how long does it take for these things to work together? Can someone **PLEASE** tell me: *At what point do we see the good?* Yes, ignorance is bliss and knowledge is painful. When you know that God is the Creator of the universe but your life is wrapped with so much pain, so many failures, so many closed doors, and so void of love, how do you handle that? How do you push past that? How do you emerge with a 'yes' still in your spirit?

I have learned that the painful transitions of life can cause one to pull away from God. There are some experiences in life that will cause you to sit by the roadside of life and make you evaluate everything. It was in such a season that I learned a shocking truth. I can only explain it by quickly referencing

Felicia C. Lucas

Ezekiel and the Valley of Dry Bones. Every time I've read this text, I've always related to Ezekiel. I've always seen the story through his eyes but one day, as I read the text with tears in my eyes, I realized I was not Ezekiel: I was the bones. I was dry. My life was dry. My relationship with God was dry. My faith was dry. My expectations were dry. My dreams were dry.

I *should've* been happily married but I was painfully divorced.

I *should've* been blissfully watching my children grow. Instead, I was struggling with parenthood.

I *should've* been in the midst of a successful career in ministry but I got lost in its politics.

My 'should haves' were replaced with "WHYS". I couldn't understand: If God loved me so much, **WHY** wasn't He coming to see about me? **WHY** wasn't He opening doors for me? **WHY** wasn't He prospering me? **WHY? WHY? WHY?** Again, too many "*WHYS*" without enough answers.

My journey has been one of loving God through my pain. It has been one of loving myself and then loving myself back to Him. It has also been one of loving Him even when I feel that He doesn't love me. In my mind, I know that He does;

Still Yes!

it just doesn't always *FEEL* like it...and that's a very real place. No one wants to talk about the fact that you know that God loves you but you don't feel it. When you see your children going astray and you've done everything you can to raise them up in the knowledge of God, it doesn't feel like He loves you. When you're losing your home, when you're losing your car, when you watch life leave the body of your loved-one, it makes you wonder: Does God care? Does He love me? Still, you know deep down on the inside that He does because He sent His Son to the cross to die for you and me. Yes, He loves me! It just doesn't always feel like it. There's peace in knowing that feelings are fickle; they are not **FACT!**

Even when it doesn't feel like it, I have to hold on to the truth that I know. I have to fight to love Him. I have to fight the voices in my head that tell me God is not real. I have to fight the voices that say, "You're praying to thin air, to nobody, and to no avail. What's the point?" I have to go through all of that and fight for my relationship with God because I love Him—and I know He loves me. So, through all the pain, brokenness, and disappointments...through the failures and shortcomings, my heart still says *"YES!"*

Felicia C. Lucas

YES, I love you, God!

YES, I'll obey You!

YES, I believe in Your Word!

YES, I'll follow You!

YES, I'll live for You!

YES, I'll serve You!

STILL YES! Through it all, my answer is *STILL* yes!

On my journey to find my way back to God, to find my way back into His love, He never stopped loving me. It was I who had to start back loving Him. I found myself reading the Bible, even when I wasn't sure I still trusted it. There were days I prayed, even when I felt no one was there; when I felt I was praying to nothing but a big, empty space in the atmosphere. I had to fight tooth and nail to get back to God. There were moments when I had to go by what I know and not by what I felt. I had to trust what I knew and what I was taught as a child growing up. I had to grab a hold of the few straws of faith I had left because my faith had been broken and shaken. It was wavering but it didn't disappear. **Now, *THAT'S* grace!**

I grabbed a hold of the few straws of faith that I had and kept holding on to those little bitty straws until they became

Still Yes!

enough for me to reach out and once again touch the Master and say, "*God, I know You're still God. I know You still sit high and look low. I know You love me. I know that You know the number of hairs on my head. I know You know the number of my days and I know that I have purpose. Despite the pain. Despite the failures. Despite the disappointments. Despite the brokenness. There's a reason You have me here, God, and I am determined to figure out what it is. I am determined to do what You created me to do and I'm determined to leave this world loving You! After all, You brought me into this world loving me.*"

I had to stop feeling, thinking, and acting like a victim. I am a conqueror! Actually, I'm **MORE** than a conqueror! I had to trust what I knew and ignore what I felt. Feelings are fickle. Truth is truth—always has been, always will be. I had to give God the same love He gives me: unconditional. I had to renew my mind and shift from "*If you do, God...*" to **"Just because You ARE God"**.

That's how I **BOUNCED BACK**. That's why **MY** answer is *STILL* **YES!**

Felicia C. Lucas

"Lord, you have been our dwelling place throughout all generations. Before the mountains were born or you brought forth the whole world, from everlasting to everlasting, you are God."

Psalm 90:1-2

THE BOUNCE BACK AUTHORS' BIOS

Felicia Lucas, the Visionary of The Bounce Back, (www.felicialucas.com) is a Minister, #1 International Best-Selling Author, Speaker, Empowerment Coach, and Publisher who passionately and enthusiastically helps individuals grow spiritually and professionally, enhance their relationships, and become wonderfully well from the inside out. Felicia, along with her husband, Pastor Kelvin Lucas, are the co-founders of *Take It By Force Ministries*, Inc. a 501(c)3 non-profit community-based youth and young adult organization, and *Dominion Tabernacle Church*. They have been married since 1997 and have three children. She is the CEO of His Glory Creations Publishing, LLC and A Moment in Time: Special Event Planning. Felicia graduated from the University of North Carolina at Chapel Hill with a B.A. Degree in Speech Communications and, for over 22 years, has worked in the Human Resources Field. She currently works as a Regional Human Resources Facilitator and Store Manager for a national retailer.

Felicia C. Lucas

Ms. Nena B. Abdul-Wakeel is a Speaker, Coach, Blogger, Podcaster, and Techie. She considers herself an Encourager. Her passion is encouraging people to see the greatness within themselves and to live their dreams. In 2017, Ms. Nena B. launched her podcast and blog, "The Ms. Nena B. Show", at www.msnenabshow.com. She uses the show as a platform to share words of wisdom, insights, and practical life tips. She loves to use her love of technology to help people learn to use it to support their dream journey. In addition to being an active member of her community and an IT manager, Ms. Nena B. is a mother of two gifted young men. She was born in Philadelphia, Pennsylvania, raised in Kansas City, Missouri, and currently resides in Silver Spring, Maryland.

The Bounce Back

Elder Lorrie Foster Crawley is a native of Warren County, North Carolina. She is married to Robert Crawley Sr. (30yrs). They were blessed with three children, Kitara, Robert Jr, and Kaylom, and one granddaughter, Kaylen. She is a member of Divine Habitation Ministries International, where she serves as Elder, Youth Coordinator, and Praise and Worship Team member. Elder Crawley is a Mentor, Teacher and Workshop Facilitator, and Entrepreneur (Events2Plan). Lorrie is the visionary for "Abba's Girls"- Daughters of the King, where women are encouraged to experience an intimate relationship with God as their Heavenly Dad. She is also the leader of the "Women of Faith Cancer Support Group", supporting women and caregivers with spiritual and emotional support during and after treatment.

Felicia C. Lucas

Vernessa Blackwell, MBA, MCLC, CJRC, CGC is an Author and Certified Grief Support and Joy Restoration Coach. The loss of both parents and all her siblings, to include three sisters and a brother, sparked her purposeful journey into coaching. Vernessa is author of *The Grief Helpline*, Mentor, Expo Host, and Speaker. Known as "The Grief Strategist", dedicated to inspiring and empowering individuals for personal and professional success, Vernessa is known for challenging and motivating clients to take action and move forward in grief and life transitions. Through coaching, training, and mentoring, she offers hope, encouragement, and support as individuals navigate the challenges and adversities of life and loss. She is the Founder of the Grief Helpline. She conducts Presentations, Workshops, In-Service Training, Assemblies, Classroom Programs, and Keynotes on topics pertaining to grief in the lives of children, teens, and adults faced with different types of loss.

The Bounce Back

Malissa Stringer is a proud graduate of Kaplan University. She holds a Master's Degree in Legal Studies, a dual Bachelor's degree in both Business/Healthcare Management and additionally, an Associates of Applied Science in Criminal Justice. Malissa is committed to developing individuals in the art of discovering their purpose and pursuing it with passion. Malissa discovered her purpose incidentally after successfully battling Breast Cancer in 2015. Since discovering her purpose, Malissa has been working on her debut work "Living Beyond Boundaries by Overcoming Obstacles", while also uplifting and encouraging others to share their gifts and talents through her motivational speeches. Malissa has had the opportunity to change the perspectives of thousands. After all, she truly believes that if you change your mind, you can change your future! Her message is simple: "Turn Obstacles into Opportunities!" Life is all about embracing our experiences and capitalizing on the opportunities they provide.

Felicia C. Lucas

Louvanta White-Horne, also known as "Cookie", is an Inspirational and Motivational Speaker and Spiritual Life Coach. She is the CEO and Founder of Refining Stepping Stones Into Beautiful Gems. Her ministry is designed to help young girls and women to bring back their self-love, not being ashamed of who they are, and embracing who they are called to be. Louvanta is very passionate about deepening her relationship with God and ministering to others. She is a proud mother of her beautiful daughter, Katrina, and also proud wife of six years to her lovely and wonderful husband, Wiley. Louvanta enjoys spending time with her family and close friends, reading, eating, dancing, shopping, and most importantly chasing after God's heart. You can connect with Louvanta on various social media platforms, to include:

Facebook: Louvanta Horne
Email: beautifulgem84@yahoo.com
Calendly.com/beautifulgem84

The Bounce Back

DuWanda S. Epps was awarded the Paul L. Stevens Humanitarian of the Year of 2017. She is the Owner of CreativeMindz Book Lounge, DSE- Determined to Succeed Everyday Magazine, 5- time Best-Selling International Author, Self-Publisher of 27 books, Co-Author of 10, Inspirational Speaker & Certified Life Coach. The Founder of (EEL) Roc'On collaborating with fellow Author and Founder of Ur Worthy Movement: Joining together to educate, empower and prevent Domestic Violence and Sexual Assault against women and men. Taking courage, strength, and faith to take a stand. Also, Founder & Operator of Cultivating Change II, Inc., a 501c3 assisting families in the community in need of clothing, food, household items, and providing resources in the community for additional services and assistance. Actor, Writer & Co-Director of Broken Silence: Play Stage.

www.creativemindzbooklounge.com
www.dsemagazine.com

Felicia C. Lucas

Melissa Bridgers-Allen is a devoted wife, mother, and family-oriented person. She is compassionate and straight-forward in every task she performs. Melissa is a Registered Nurse, specializing in providing care for terminally-ill patients and educating families. She loves the Lord and believes in serving others.

The Bounce Back

Rayshoun Chambers has successfully held senior leadership positions within best-in-class organizations, including First Data, Elavon, and WorldPay U.S. As the Founder, CEO of RAC Venture Group, LLC., her company brings Six Sigma methodologies to small companies and corporations resulting in project and program movement from concept to cash flow. As an Author, Payments Professional, fierce Coach, proud mom, lover of Christ, and loyal friend, she fashions herself a lifetime student. The drive she garnered over the years allows her to push past NO's for the YES just on the other side. Rayshoun has recently become increasingly sought after for speaking engagements, collaborations, and professional projects – the likes of which she cheerfully participates if the alignment is right. You can follow her on Twitter @RayshounC.

Felicia C. Lucas

Pastor Shamielle Alston is uniqueness walking. Her story is one of survival. Difficult doesn't begin to describe her life as a foster child but God had plans for her that she herself couldn't imagine. Her childhood simply molded her for those plans. A breath of fresh air, Pastor Alston delivers inspirational messages that expose listeners to God's love for them. Pastor Alston's story will bring you to tears and joy. It will unravel questions of doubt concerning God's love for us while also ensuring its validity. Her philosophy is that everyone needs to know that God loves them, and it's her job to tell them. Using her speaking ministry, drama, writing, and music, she does just that. Pastor Alston is a treasure to all whom meet her.

The Bounce Back

Sharlrita Deloatch assists working women who know there's more to life meant for them than their 9 to 5 or their job in becoming successful business owners. As the "Secret Weapon" for women, she provides proven, exclusive strategies and tips to help them build a solid foundation in their business. Sharlrita is no stranger to making bad choices in life. She captivates her audiences about her journey *From Convicted Felon to Thriving Entrepreneur*. Sharlrita chooses to use her Pain to Propel her into her purpose through speaking, writing, and coaching other women to do the same. With her demanding approach to living on purpose, she makes a great impact on the lives of individuals and corporations each time she opens her mouth. Sharlrita used her pain of not being able to "find a job" by leveraging the 15 years of customer service experience and started her own Customer Service Consulting Company "New Phase Career Solutions" where they help small businesses and non-profits improve their bottom line profitability by teaching, training and providing strategies so that the company can provide the best customer service to each client every time.

Felicia C. Lucas

Reflections

www.ingramcontent.com/pod-product-compliance
Lightning Source LLC
Chambersburg PA
CBHW071523080526
44588CB00011B/1535